Win ’Em Over

Leadership Planners Series

Future-Proof Your Team

Win 'Em Over

Leadership Planners

Win 'Em Over

CATHERINE HAKALA-AUSPERK

ALA Editions
CHICAGO | 2019

CATHERINE HAKALA-AUSPERK is an author and national library speaker and consultant. She teaches at Kent State University's iSchool, as well as for the American Library Association's Certified Public Library Administrator (CPLA) program, and many other organizations. She is the author of *Renew Yourself: A Six-Step Plan for More Meaningful Work, Build a Great Team: One Year to Success, Be a Great Boss: One Year to Success,* and this Leadership Planners series. Her passions are for supporting, coaching, and developing great libraries, successful teams, and—especially—strong and effective library leaders. You can follow her on Facebook at www.facebook.com/librariesthrive or on her website, librariesthrive.com.

ISBN: 978-0-8389-1811-1 (paper)

Library of Congress Cataloging in Publication Control Number: 2018050553

Book design by Alejandra Diaz in the Expo Serif Pro and Fira Sans typefaces.

∞ This paper meets the requirements of ANSI/NISO Z39.48–1992 (Permanence of Paper).

Printed in the United States of America
23 22 21 20 19 5 4 3 2 1

ALA Editions purchases fund advocacy, awareness, and accreditation programs for library professionals worldwide.

For my grandkids.
When you think you can't do something,
whatever it is, you can.

Contents

AUTHOR'S NOTE

There are more of these leadership planners in the works. You can help make each one better than the next! Please send your feedback, criticism, suggestions, and topic ideas to me. What kind of leadership success would you like to plan?

chakalaausperk@gmail.com

It wasn't raining when Noah built the ark.

—RICHARD CUSHING

Why Plan?

NO ONE PLANS TO FAIL BUT, ODDLY ENOUGH, FEW PEOPLE PLAN TO SUCCEED. Using the planners in this series, you can do just that.

Planners are making a comeback (if they ever really went away). Even though we have high-tech tools we can use to chart our lives, today's planners are bright and engaging. Why use them? There are as many answers as there are lines on which to write.

Planners, experts tell us, can help us get and stay organized, make more intentional choices, be more productive, waste less time, reduce stress, and provide the time and tools that can help us solve today's challenges.

These planners are designed for library leaders who are facing some pretty serious challenges but haven't even had the chance to close their doors, sit back, untangle their issues, and begin to think about how to make things better.

Write in this book. Think of it as a combination to-do list, diary, and surrogate hairdresser or bartender (or any other good listener) that can provide you with the space, advice, and the luxury of time to think things through.

By the time you've finished all the readings and exercises, you will not have solved your problems. But you will be ready to *start* solving them—*and* you'll have a plan to do so.

Be so good
they can't ignore you.

—STEVE MARTIN

Win 'Em Over

A NEW DIRECTOR recently shared her frustration after attending a board dinner at a local restaurant, during which the board president turned to her and asked, "Are you sure you're old enough to drink?" Sound familiar? Or, have you heard about the problems the new branch manager is having now that he must supervise peers he's been friends with for years? Or maybe you can relate to the new dean who offers one new idea after the other, only to be met with, "Oh, honey, we've been doing this a lot longer than you have and we *know* that won't work here!"

No matter how talented a leader you are, there are often barriers in your way caused by a lack of trust or respect, or more likely an absence of confidence. Yours *and* theirs. You can plan to overcome that!

By reading and completing this planner, you can examine the implications, the challenges, and the solutions that confidence—or a lack thereof—can bring. One thing is certain. The doubters probably won't change, but you can. By trusting yourself and by convincing others of your skills and abilities, you can *win 'em over*—and plan to succeed!

Let today be the day
you give up who you've been
for who you can become.

—HAL ELROD

Plan to Establish Yourself

WHEN I WAS a sophomore journalism major, all of nineteen years old, I applied for and was offered the position of writer for my university's public relations office. I had one writing class under my belt so, hey, that made me a writer, didn't it? I was pretty sure I could do the job.

Years later, I was again offered a position I was pretty sure I could do. *Pretty sure.* And that worked out okay, too. Lucky break or confident decision? Who knows? What I do know is that during the early months in these positions and in many others, I probably wasn't the only one who was just *pretty sure.* Mark Twain assured us that the concept of an overnight success doesn't really exist. As a matter of fact, he's often quoted as saying it once took him three weeks to prepare an impromptu speech! Comedian Eddie Cantor estimated that becoming an *overnight success* took him at least twenty years.

How about you? Whether you are brand new to your position or if you've been at it for a while, do you still have doubts about your abilities, your decision-making, or maybe if you should even be sitting in that chair? Although others may share these common suspicions, that doesn't help much. As you've read in the introduction to this planner, being mocked or questioned because of your age (be it young or old), your appearance, your background, or even your abilities, can severely chip away at whatever level of confidence you already have—until and unless you establish yourself. You can start today.

To paraphrase some advice shared by Harrison Kratz on workitdaily.com, there are five great ideas for getting started. (I'd say there really are six, because the first and most important is to never stop believing in yourself.)

Kratz recommends that you begin by:

1. Finding out who has the real power (who may not always be the most obvious people) and win them over.
2. Don't keep your past accomplishments a secret—share your background.
3. Build fabulous communication skills, including when to talk and when to listen.
4. Strive to understand how—and why—your team thinks and acts the way they do.
5. Commit to building respectful and professional relationships (and that takes time!).

Victories

You've undoubtedly already achieved several victories that have helped you strengthen your confidence in yourself. Describe them, from the simplest to your greatest confidence builder thus far. Then sit back, read them again, and let them be the impetus to keep you going!

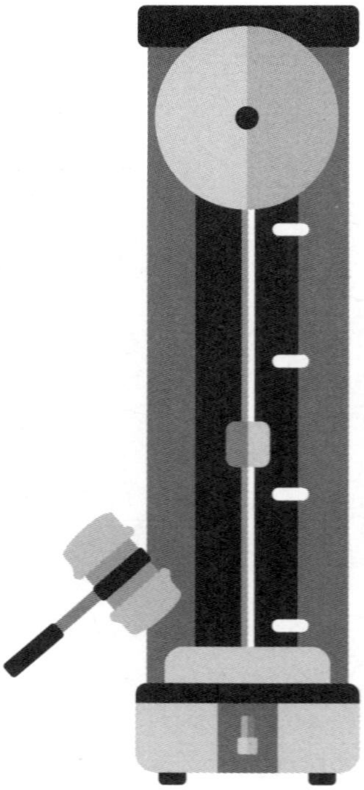

Greatest Confidence Builder So Far

This One Surprised Even Me

Tougher Challenge

Easy Victory

IMPOSTER SYNDROME

So, you see, we were right—we could do it! What is important to remember is that before we can begin demonstrating the confidence others have in us, we must start by believing in the confidence we build in ourselves.

Informatics and journalism librarian Willie Miller of Indiana University—Purdue University Indianapolis refers to this as avoiding the "imposter syndrome." His advice to recover from this malady? Convince yourself that you belong in every room. Because, quite simply, you do! If that sounds easier said than done, keep reading.

Anka Wittenberg, a guest writer for Entrepreneur.com, offers some concrete steps that you can use to continue to build your own confidence, whether you're so new you don't know where to park or you've been around so long you can't even remember what you did before.

1. One of my mentors used to call this first tip "raise your hand." Wittenberg describes it as getting out of your comfort zone and pushing yourself to try something new. So, volunteer for something brand new, something that will help you stretch a bit. That will always wake you up! However, to feel like you're on safe footing, be sure that when you are stretching your skills you are still matching your interests.

2. In the 1980 classic movie *Caddyshack,* the character played by Chevy Chase encourages a young golfer to "be the ball." Wittenberg echoes this concept but calls it "visualizing." In other words, you need to practice seeing your own success. For example, if you want to be an administrator, behave, work, train, and act as though you already are.
3. The next tip is to know what you're already good at. And don't guess—be certain. While people are usually loath to toot their own horns, you still need to acknowledge and demonstrate what you're good at, even when you're busy learning new skills. These are the baby steps you'll build on.
4. Finally, if you act according to your values—always—those with similar values will be drawn to you. At the same time, you'll be demonstrating honesty and consistency, both of which build trust.

Taking the Temperature

Take a snapshot of where you feel your confidence levels are today. First, draw a needle on each dial as a measurement (0 for low, 10 for high). Then, in each category, comment honestly about why you feel you are at this level and what you can do to move the needle up.

Confidence in Myself	Team Confidence in Me	Supervisor Confidence in Me	Colleagues' Confidence in Me

BE THE BALL

Let's get back to the future for a moment (pun intended). By reading and completing this planner, you will be plotting some specific, targeted changes you'll make to increase both your confidence in yourself and others' confidence in you. But, to what end? Before you get too far down this road, make sure you know where it is leading. If you don't know where you're going, how will you know when you've arrived?

How do you see yourself at the end of your career? How about at the end of this week? Likely, the answer is the same. We all have a vision of what and whom we want to be and hope that others will see us just that way. I've never met anyone who wants to just stumble through life, bending whichever way the wind blows, with everyone (including you) wondering what will happen next. Okay, maybe some people end up like that, but I doubt they planned to.

The End in Sight

Complete this Lifetime Achievement Award certificate by describing your confident, successful self exactly as you want others to see you, both now and in the future. Then, have the confidence to make this happen.

LIFETIME ACHIEVEMENT AWARD

~ This Is to Recognize ~

____

1. ______________________________

____

2. ______________________________

____

3. ______________________________

____

4. ______________________________

____

SMALL VICTORIES

You've probably heard the advice that when you're planning to get all the apples off the tree, start with the low-hanging fruit. Basically, that means to start small. Don't get me wrong, I'm all for BHAGS (Big, Hairy, Audacious Goals)! But I'm also a fan of small victories along the way. Personally, I have every intention to write the Great American Novel. Still, I started with newspaper stories, then worked up to columns, then chapters, some freelancing, and now books like this one. My Great American Novel, written mostly in pencil on the back of restaurant placemats (I was a waitress when I started it), still sits next to me and I will finish it. Just not today.

So, give yourself a break. You likely won't, to paraphrase Dale Carnegie, win new friends and influence all people overnight. But you most certainly can begin to move closer to your own *lifetime achievement* vision of confidence and professional success—one day at a time. The secret is to never stop believing in yourself and leave frustration and negativity behind.

This is a simple piece of advice that's worth repeating. As you begin this effort, make sure you surround yourself with positive people and immerse yourself in positive experiences. In my book *Be a Great Boss: One Year to Success,* I said it this way: *Don't hang around with dead people.* Negativity can be like a wet paperback in a book drop that shares its ick and odor with everything it touches. You're visioning, remember? You can see the strong and confident professional you seek to become. Don't let anyone or anything get in the way of achieving that vision.

Experience doesn't
come with age.
Experience comes with
doing things, trying things,
or even thinking things.

—JAMES BLACKER

Plan to Work Well with the More Experienced

EVERY TIME WE were about to get a new manager, one of my former colleagues would say he hoped they didn't send some young whippersnapper who was going to come in all positive and energetic and tell us we were doing everything wrong! Even though those characteristics could be demonstrated by someone of any age, he was clearly focusing on youth.

However, sometimes long-time team members have a certain attitude about new managers, no matter their age, based solely on the fact that the new person is, well, new. And they're not! They have a proprietary sense of ownership of existing policies and practices, most likely because they helped to create them. For that reason alone, they just might take *any* suggestion of change as a personal challenge, and that's not going to do much for the confidence of the new leader.

If you walk into a room where team members are working and suddenly the room goes quiet, you can't help but wonder what problem they have with you. The longer you wait to figure it out or pretend it doesn't bother you (and it will), the more damage you'll do to your own confidence. You have options that will help you understand their impressions of you. So, consider them. One by one, reflect on your interactions with each person and identify any issues you've had. Once known, they can be overcome.

Most important, believe what you see, not what you hear. Among the sage advice on supervising those who have been around longer than you, the editor of *The Muse* suggests you immediately dismiss three common misconceptions.

1. Don't believe that you just can't relate to some people or they to you, because you can. Just picture the different people of all ages you connect with outside of work. You can do it at work, too.
2. Don't believe you can't learn from others just because they do things the old way. In a strong team, people of all ages and backgrounds learn from one another.
3. Don't believe everyone learns the same way—even if what they're learning is to get used to you. Strive to understand—and relate to—their differences, just as they do with yours.

What's the Catch?

For each category, put a dot on the number that reflects where on a scale of 1 to 10 most of your team would rate you *right now*. Then, no matter the number, under each heading write at least two concrete things you can do to raise that number. Also, draw a line connecting the dots to show where you are now overall, then come back in about a year and do this exercise again. Your numbers (and your line graph) should be a lot higher!

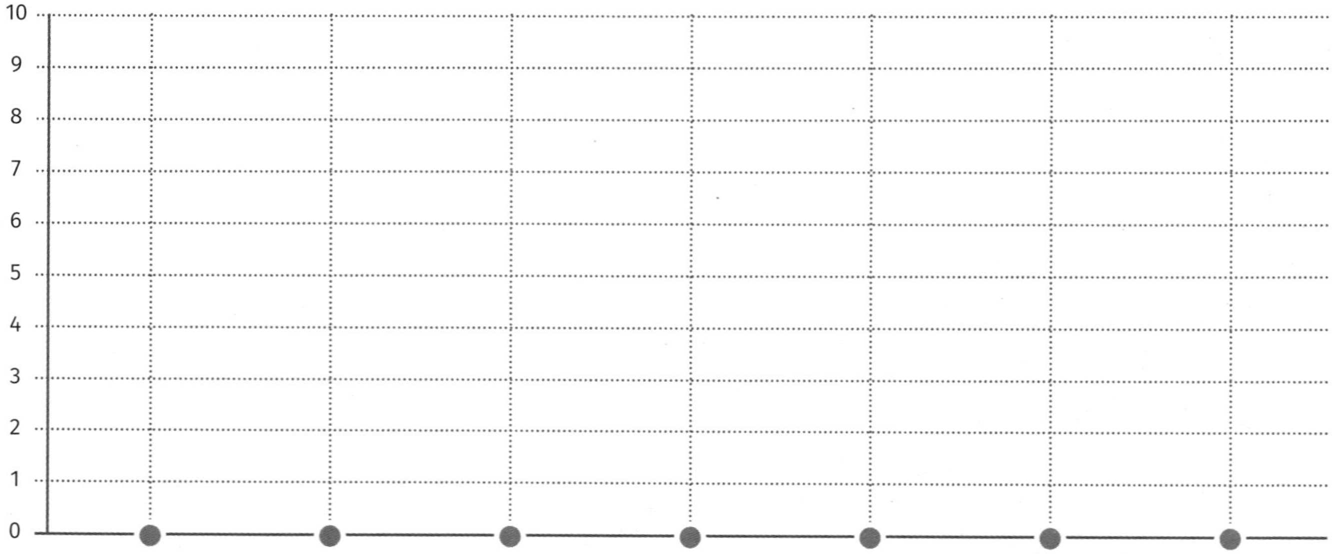

Honesty	Your Respect for Them	Their Respect Level for You	How Much You Appreciate the Team	The Value of Your Experience	Recognition of Your Knowledge and Skills	Your Understanding of Each Team Member

OLD IS THE NEW YOUNG

It's easy to say and to believe that managing people is always the same, no matter their ages or levels of expertise. But that's just not true. Each person's unique background brings layers of experience that can enforce or erode everything from trust to attitude to performance. You're the leader now, so you need to get to work unravelling it all.

By reflecting on some advice from EmploymentCrossing.com, you can get a great start by putting some real, practical tips to work right away.

- ✓ I've never yet met a newborn baby who knows how to be a good leader. Leadership is a skill. Skills are learned. Sure, some soft skills are inborn or are part of a personality, but other parts of a tough job take effort and intention to master. Learn, study, read, and never stop. Not only will your confidence grow, but those around you will see and admire the steps you are taking to improve.

Build a Bigger Trophy Case

List at least four projects or accomplishments you can use to build a bond with one or more colleagues who have more experience than you. Describe projects you can work on together, right now, that can be successful not in spite of, but because of, your combined talents, as well as the confidence you'll build in one another.

2

3

1

4

- ✓ Walking down the hall one morning after just landing an assistant administrator position, I was surprised to hear the director on the phone, asking someone for advice. Somehow, in my naiveté, I had assumed directors were directors because they already knew everything! But that day, I learned the smart ones get help. Be smart. Ask for help when you need it.
- ✓ Maybe you know what people are saying about you. Or you've heard rumors. If so, take that chip off your shoulder and leave it in your car. Walk into your leadership position, whether new or not, with no baggage that could negatively affect you and get to work. Pretty soon, you'll like what people are saying.
- ✓ Finally, don't apologize for doing what must be done, especially if that means responding to a negative attitude with a rebuke or even with discipline. Be the leader, good or bad. Consistency builds confidence all around.

RESPECTING THE PAST, EMBRACING THE FUTURE

Why didn't someone tell you *that* was about to happen? What's going on with the reference desk schedule? Why did the director give that new assignment to someone else? What were people just talking about in the staff room? Uncertainty creates a vacuum that is often filled with fear (both yours and theirs). And, for you, there's nothing that breeds negativity more than wondering how you can possibly be successful as a leader without the support of a team that you can trust.

But wait, you may have just jumped to an unwarranted conclusion.

Although you and your team may not see eye to eye *yet*, that doesn't mean they don't have proud and storied achievements behind them that you can both build upon. Just look at all they've done before you arrived, or at least before you took the helm. No, really, take the time to look. Undoubtedly, at one point or another, they've shown loyalty, achievement, teamwork, and even demonstrated understanding, acceptance, and confidence to fellow team members and previous leaders of all stripes. You just need to give the relationship you're building time to grow.

There's one more thing you can do to move that building process along. Acknowledge all the achievements you've just unearthed. Congratulate your team. Recognize them for their contributions, and then remind them of how much more you will be able to achieve together.

Blending a successful past with a promising future is a confidence builder for everyone. Even if you're still looking through a veil of newness and uncertainty, at least you're building experiences—together.

When you're in jail,
a good friend will be trying
to bail you out.
A best friend will be in the
cell next to you.

—GROUCHO MARX

Plan to Supervise Friends

As the manager stepped up to the office door, she paused with her hand on the knob. She knew who was in there. A friend. Someone she'd worked alongside, had fun with, and complained with for many years. Heck, they'd even been in each other's weddings! But, today, she wasn't just a friend, she was also the boss. And this was going to be a very tough conversation about performance issues. How, exactly, was she supposed to pull this off?

IF THIS SITUATION sounds familiar to you, then you've likely faced this type of challenge before. Internal promotions are common, and in some libraries, they're the accepted, and sometimes only, career path that's offered. What that means is we often end up supervising people we've known, worked alongside, and commiserated with for years. A new relationship can succeed, but it's going to take time and a strong self-image to assume this new role and to build their confidence that you can pull it off.

I would suggest that there are some measures you can take to make the transition from buddy to boss successful by expanding on some advice offered by Monster.com career expert Vicki Salemi. Through intentional, professional actions you can become more confident in your new role every day. As your confidence grows, so will their confidence in you. It's hard to trust someone whose knees are knocking! Unless you trust yourself, it will be difficult, if not impossible, for you to earn their confidence in you as a leader.

DISENGAGE

"I can still go out to have a drink with my old friends when we're not working, right? I mean, I don't have to stop being their friend, do I?" The quick and tough answer to that is *yes, you do*. But, it is a somewhat qualified answer. While perhaps being best friends isn't going to work, you can continue to be close colleagues—and still be able to do your respective jobs well. The truth is, as the leader of the people whom you once considered equals, you're going to have to keep a bit of distance so that you can engage in a more *professional* type of friendship. It might look and feel like there's less of a connection. That's because—at work—there is. Depending on the culture of your organization (and often its size) you may have to drop out of the bowling league, give up poker night, or even skip those payday lunches. Unless, of course, you do all these activities with a group of your team members and not just the ones with whom you were close friends.

Don't worry. Some things—the important things—will stay the same. Good friends care about each other's success, support each other in times of challenge, and share each other's joys. Professional colleagues can do the same—just by using a slightly different approach.

Evolutions

Translate the relationship you've built over the years into a new form that allows you and a friend to work confidently as supervisor and supervisee. In the first column, write something you did or said that demonstrated each characteristic when you were just colleagues. Now, as your professional relationship evolves, how might the examples change, even though the qualities of your relationship remain the same? Write these answers in column 2.

	As Friends	Boss/Report
Respect		
Understanding		
Support		
Encouragement		
Trust		

SET THE TONE

Understanding what professional relationships are supposed to look like is one thing, but seriously, how do you make them work? As both a professional and a leader, it's likely you already know the answer because it would be the same one you'd use to institute a new policy or procedure. With people, though, it needs to be tweaked just a bit to be more human. Still, similar guidelines still apply. Two of the most important might be:

- Start with ground rules. Whether presented in a team meeting, which is always preferred because it allows everyone to hear the same thing at the same time, or discussed one on one, say the ground rules out loud. Then, write them down. Then, post them. And, finally, follow and enforce them. What will the culture or personality of the workplace you lead be like? What behavior will be allowed and what will not? A brand-new director once found herself in a work environment that thrived on gossip, sarcasm, and criticism. Unwilling to work in such a place, she called a meeting and spent the morning filling flip chart pages with ground rules that would support a respectful and professional environment. Afterward, several team members thanked her for cleaning the place up. They explained they had been finding it tough just to show up, but now they'd feel safer.
- Don't keep expectations secret! (See above...say out loud, write, post, follow.) What do you expect from your team and when do you expect it? A popular Food Network cooking competition throws a wrench into a project with only minutes remaining. Do you plan to do that? If you do, warn them. If not, tell them! If possible, share up front the criteria on which team members will be evaluated so they can see that you will be consistent and fair—to everyone. And don't forget to ask the most important question: What do they expect from you? You need honesty and dependability to build confidence—and it needs to come from both sides.

Here's a worthwhile way to spend part of a staff meeting that will help you understand the answer to that important question. Have your team members complete the **Memories** exercise. Using this information, you'll see what your team expects you to do to get into that *best boss* category. Do the exercise yourself just to see how revealing it can be.

RESPECT BOUNDARIES

Some practical advice that has proven valuable over the years is, when you must sit down and have a very difficult conversation begin by saying, "We need to have a very difficult conversation." The same advice can work for setting boundaries. Why? Because it's easy to slip back into what's comfortable or what used to be acceptable under the previous boss. Perhaps more aptly, *especially* when things

Memories

Close your eyes. Really. Close them! Now, think back to the best boss you ever had. Write down at least ten ways that boss made you feel about yourself and about your job. Now, close your eyes again and (sorry about this, but . . .) remember the worst boss you ever had. In the second bubble, write down those feelings and your resulting work performance.

Don't apologize. When it's time to take a tougher stance and things get more serious, do your job. You've laid enough honest groundwork so that your *friends* should not be surprised that, after all, you're just doing the job they're becoming confident you can do.

BEST Boss Ever

1. ______
2. ______
3. ______
4. ______
5. ______
6. ______
7. ______
8. ______
9. ______
10. ______

WORST Boss Ever

1. ______
2. ______
3. ______
4. ______
5. ______
6. ______
7. ______
8. ______
9. ______
10. ______

start slipping backward, no matter how much it might sting, putting up the stop sign quickly might be the best option. Try saying, "We need to stop this right now and respect the new boundaries we've established."

So long as you've clarified your mutual respect and your new relationship remains intact, both of you might be more confident of where you now stand. Be prepared, though. As is the case with so much of leadership, this sounds a bit easier than it is.

> *The whole staff had been hearing stories for years about a staff member's marriage being on the rocks. Even before you became boss, you'd also heard it all. But recently, things seemed to be getting worse. Almost every lunch break was filled with uncomfortable details of the relationship's steady demise. What used to just be sad and difficult for you to hear was now far too personal to be professionally appropriate to hear as a boss. When your staff member came into the office this morning, closed the door, and began, "Wait until you hear what happened now," you decided enough was enough. It had to stop.*

How would you begin that conversation with someone you care deeply about? Would you have the confidence to speak the truth? Would you be able to say something like, "The staff is talking about us? You're in here too often with the door closed. We have to respect new boundaries?" I'm certain there's one thing you're sure about—you'd need the confidence of a leader to make this right. Or maybe it would work the other way. Once you made this right, you'd then *have* the confidence of a professional leader!

Keeping Your Balance

To maintain a professional balance that will allow your team to be confident in your fair and unbiased leadership, describe in each space on the right several things you might do to ensure that the situations in the opposite box will exist.

Support All Team Members Equally

Keep No Inappropriate Secrets

Maintain Professional Social Connections

Show No Favoritism

Maintain Professional Boundaries

You cannot be a leader, and
ask other people to follow you,
unless you know how
to follow, too.

—SAM RAYBURN

Plan to Follow Well

QUITE OFTEN, IT'S helpful to have the right words or phrases ready to use in awkward situations. We learn this in our many "How to Deal with Challenging Patrons" trainings, don't we? When it comes to being a good follower, there's one expression to always have handy. A mentor once shared with me that, if you find yourself in the boss's office and she is upset about something you've done, don't waste time denying, justifying, or even admitting the mistake. Instead, get right to the solution. As in, *what do you want to happen?* If we want to be followed, we need to learn to follow as well, and to be a good follower, we must first understand exactly what our own boss needs from us. We've accepted the position. Now, we must do the job.

If you would prefer to skip that whole uncomfortable office-visit thing altogether, then you should be asking yourself that same question every day: *what do you want to happen?* Why? Because for your boss to have confidence in you, you need to convince her that her trust is well placed. How can you do that? By working to support her goals—as well as your own. Here are just a couple of ways you can demonstrate that she can trust you to follow as well as to lead:

- **Do your job.** Your boss needs you to do whatever it is you have been tasked with doing. There's a reason you've been asked to do it. Quite possibly, it fits into a larger picture and, if you can't come through on your end, she will have much bigger problems down the road.
- **Solve, don't share, problems.** There are those supervisors whose standard retort to any challenge is, "It's up to the boss." Or, "Let me check with the boss." Guess what? The boss likely doesn't want to hear about it. What she wants to hear instead is silence—or the sound of work that's getting done because you made the necessary decisions and solved the problems yourself.
- **Bring ideas, not complaints.** Sometimes, you must float something upstairs. You can just feel in your bones that the final decision's a little over your pay grade. That's okay, so long as you remember to present the situation as a potential solution and not just as a challenging problem to drop in your boss's lap!
- **Leave your personal life at home.** The personal and the professional should not mix. Period.

I've Got Your Back

Your boss needs to be confident in your support in all these areas. Write several things you will do, that you haven't done before, to clearly demonstrate your support in each area.

- **Pretend that everyone you hire will be with your library for a minimum of thirty years, whether they turn out to be good hires or bad.** So, make sure you develop the skills you need to hire the right ones the first time.
- **Go along to get along.** Today, we work together. Departments, libraries, even cities need to blend people into teams that can collaborate, share, and get along. Your boss needs to be confident that you can be trusted to make friends, to acquiesce once in a while, to compromise, and to build partnerships that can benefit the library.

"FOLLOWING" LANGUAGE

Maybe you've been in a situation like this or, if not, you can probably imagine it . . .

Your boss comes into the department meeting and shares some news that no one on the team wants to hear. You know that program on world religions that everyone was so excited about, the one you've all worked for months to put together? Well, she just cancelled it. Why? Because apparently [major eye roll at this point], someone [insert a dismissive nod here, pointed in the general direction of the director's office] has decided it's too political since everyone's arguing about religion and because there's a bond issue on the ballot the day after the program was scheduled to take place. Questions start coming right away. "What about the first amendment?" someone asks. "Don't we believe in intellectual freedom anymore?" asks another. Your boss's answer is the clincher: "Don't ask me! It wasn't my decision!"

First of all, that's the wrong thing to say. There are many wrong things to say and just as many wrong ways to say them *if* you're still trying to build your boss's confidence in you as a leader.

Sometimes it's hard to just barely hang onto the edge of the bandwagon without falling off. You can make it easier by saying the right things in the right way. For example:

- **Consistency builds confidence.** Your boss needs to know that, whatever the new decision is, you will respond to it and to her with clarity, thoughtfulness, support, and respect. Always.

In Other Words

As a confident leader who has the full trust of your supervisor, translate each of these comments into language a good follower might use to say the same thing in a way that is more positive and supportive.

"It Wasn't My Decision"	____________________
"Nobody Asked Me"	____________________
"I Have No Idea What Might Happen"	____________________
"They Never Tell Me Anything"	____________________
"It's Above My Pay Grade"	____________________
"Nothing We Can Say Would Matter at This Point"	____________________

- **Honesty builds confidence.** Your boss also needs to know that if you do disagree, you won't be afraid to speak your piece privately and directly, and to offer alternatives that are reasonable and relevant.
- **Support builds confidence.** Your boss needs to be certain that once you walk out of the office door to deliver news to your team, you'll be on board and will support her decisions and actions 100 percent. Effective leaders—and teams—speak with one voice. When you back your boss, you'll also have the confidence to know she'll back you.

BE A CONFIDENT FOLLOWER

Think back to one of the first times you found yourself called to the boss's office for what promised to be not just a social visit. What were you thinking and feeling? For many, as they reached for that doorknob or sat in front of that big desk nervously tapping their foot, there were a variety of things running through their minds. *I don't belong here, I didn't do anything wrong. I know I did something wrong, I wonder what it was. I knew I would never pull this job off. She isn't going to believe a word I say. What if I just can't do it? That's it. I'm fired.* This planner is all about enhancing the confidence others have in you and you have in yourself. There's no escaping the fact that to do either successfully, you're going to have to keep positive thoughts. Consider, then, these alternatives.

- *I don't belong here.* It's worth reminding you of Miller's comments in the "Plan to Establish Yourself" section of this text. Remember? He referred to this as the "imposter syndrome" and responded to it by claiming that yes, you *do* belong in every room you enter. That's a good place to start.
- *I'll never pull this job off.* Start doing the part of the job you know and fill in your time by learning the parts that you don't. Often, a commitment to learning new skills can be seen as just as valuable a trait as having those skills to begin with.
- *She isn't going to believe a word I say.* First, you need to believe in what you say, and the best way to do that is to be consistently honest. *Always.* Someone once said it's dangerous to start lying about your age because, as the years go by, the math gets harder.
- *What if I just can't do it?* Obviously, that's a possibility. And it's one that should never be seen as representing weakness or failure. But save it for last after trying absolutely everything else. One of the most successful, driven, and well-recognized staff trainers I've ever known spent one miserable year as a branch manager before she admitted she just couldn't do that job. It just wasn't for her. It wasn't that she couldn't be successful—she just couldn't be successful *there.* When she moved back into her training coordinator role, she was successful beyond measure!

You can't build
a reputation on what
you are going to do.

—HENRY FORD

Plan to Contribute

FREQUENTLY, AFTER BEING passed over for promotion, applicants would come to me and ask, "Why? Why not me? I've come to work every day and done exactly what was asked of me!" And there was the answer. Doing only what you're expected to do is why you get a paycheck. To move up, it's necessary to do more.

To be respected or, better yet, admired, we need to reach beyond standard performance expectations, take risks, and tackle even bigger challenges. Catherine Monnin, a friend and mentor, often shared this advice in career advancement workshops: to be recognized as a leader you really only have to do one thing: *raise your hand*. And you need to do it over and over and over. What she meant was: step up, accept a challenge, take a risk that no one else is willing to take. Be the person others see as a positive and innovative force that can move everyone forward.

I know what you're thinking. This advice is contrary to that of the experts who tell us to learn when to say "No!" Or maybe you're remembering that multitasking is out of fashion these days. Or perhaps you're simply wondering when you're going to sleep. Author Curt Rosengren can help. He suggests that there is a litmus test of sorts to help assure that you're raising your hand for the right reason. These reasons, he suggests, are worthy of someone who truly wants to contribute something that matters. So, ask yourself:

- Will my taking this on have a direct impact on my library (or my career)?
- Is this a positive-focused activity?
- Does this offer an opportunity to share knowledge with someone else?
- Will this activity foster a stronger community?

Plan to do much more than just what's expected of you. Plan to contribute in a long-term, impactful way so that the reputation you're attempting to establish (or enhance) is worth emulating. But remember that there's a greater danger in *not* keeping a promise than there is reward for doing so. So be sure that when you do raise your hand, you're going to be able to come through and do what you've said you'll do.

Birds on a Wire

Perhaps you've heard the one about the five birds on a wire? Three said they were going to fly away. How many were left? Two? No. Five. They just *said* they were going to fly away. They didn't really do it. No one is perfect. We've all made well-intentioned but unkept promises. Often, the first step toward avoiding such pitfalls is to recognize what can go wrong in the first place and to plan ways around it. Fill in these four boxes with projects, ideas, duties, or just dreams you said you would complete . . . but haven't yet. Explain why not—and what you're going to do now to complete them.

Unfinished Promise/Project

____

____

What Got in the Way?

____

____

____

I'll Get around This Hurdle by . . .

____

____

____

Unfinished Promise/Project

____

____

What Got in the Way?

____

____

____

I'll Get around This Hurdle by . . .

____

____

____

Unfinished Promise/Project

____

____

What Got in the Way?

____

____

____

I'll Get around This Hurdle by . . .

____

____

____

Unfinished Promise/Project

____

____

What Got in the Way?

____

____

____

I'll Get around This Hurdle by . . .

____

____

____

Promises You Will Keep

Projects get completed, promises are kept, and trust is built one step at a time. Pick just one of the projects you listed in the **Birds on a Wire** exercise that you still want to accomplish and fill in all the steps—both large and small—as well as all the real deadlines that will help you do so.

PROJECT

____

____

____

Check When Finished	To Do	By When?
☐		
☐		
☐		
☐		
☐		
☐		
☐		
☐		
☐		
☐		

USE MISSION AS YOUR GUIDE

You may have heard of this strategic process before: it's called *cascading*. One of the most frequent complaints about the value of strategic planning is that it's so high-level that it often means nothing to those on the front line. One solution is to cascade your library's mission and goals down through every department and branch. This is another way to make sure that your contributions are focused, relevant, and valuable to your organization. Here's an example of how cascading might work for you:

- ***Your library's mission***—We enhance community life.
- ***Your library's goal***—We will remain aware of residents' needs.

You just spent three days redesigning your library's timecards. Does that effort in any way enhance your community's life? (Answer: NO) Next week, you're planning to spend some time preparing to lead the book discussion group. It is no longer a part of your job description, but you've done it for so many years that you just hate to give it up. Will that reading, research, and question writing help you better understand your residents' needs? (Answer again: NO)

Okay, so maybe there are more strategic ways you could be spending your time. And, just maybe, they would not only better support your library, but also help to build and grow the confidence others have in you.

Consider this:

- *(In support of your library's mission)* ***Your mission***—I will review all personnel work assignments, making sure they either enhance the community's life in some way or are discontinued or modified.
- *(In support of your library's goal)* ***One of your goals***—I will work with staff to design an ongoing suggestion program that will encourage and collect resident input both on paper and virtually.

PLAN TO CONTRIBUTE TO YOUR OWN SUCCESS, TOO!

Leaders grow. To keep your own skills sharp and to model what lifelong learning and achievement really look like, you're going to have to remain committed to your own improvement as well as your team's and your library's. It's simple, really. You can use the same tools and process!

- At the same time each year, take a full day to focus on your own growth.
- Summarize what you hope to achieve in the coming year by writing your own mission statement. This simple statement should answer the question: "Why will you continue to work in this profession this year?"

- Identify as many things that must happen as you can think of for your mission to be achieved. Then, remembering that you only have one year, select no more than three as your goals.
- Consider what reaching each goal will take. Those will be your objectives.
- Explore, research, and reach out to find opportunities to learn, to stretch, to follow, or otherwise be inspired to become a better leader.
- Don't sit on the wire. Put down some active steps, with honest time lines and deadlines, that you'll take to achieve those objectives.
- Repeat at the same time next year.

Now you have a strategy to make real contributions to your own career, in support of your library and to continue to build confidence in your leadership and *Win 'Em Over!*

It takes 20 years to build
a reputation and
5 minutes to ruin it.
If you think about that,
you'll do things differently.

—WARREN BUFFETT

Plan to Win a Few . . . and Lose a Few

A FORMER LIBRARY school instructor and mentor of mine was often heard giving this sage (if not civil) advice when teaching future managers how to be effective leaders. First, he'd warn them that they were going to need to make a lot of decisions. He'd explain that people would be depending on them to make those decisions, some of which might be especially difficult or unpopular. "Don't worry about whether you're making the right decision or the wrong decision," he'd caution, "Just make a damn decision!"

While it might often seem like a contradiction in terms, you can sometimes gain the trust and confidence of your team by doing the opposite of what they want you to do. Why? Because at least you're doing *something*. You're trying, you're making your best guess, you're moving the group and organization forward, and whatever the result, you'll stand behind it. But all that doesn't make it any easier to be the most unpopular one in the room.

So, that's how it's going to go? Good days and bad days? Pretty much. But you're not in this leadership thing for the short term, right? Remember where you started this journey. As a leader, you found yourself surrounded by those who had little confidence in you. Maybe they thought you were too young or too inexperienced or just too unlike them to lead them. Maybe they questioned whether you had the nerve to do what needed to be done? Everything you've considered so far has been designed to relieve them of those misconceptions. Complete the **Walking the Plank** exercise so that you'll be ready for a few, small setbacks.

But move forward you will. There's no shortage of advice out there on how to win people over (and you should avail yourself of as much of it as possible). Here are some key points that stand out:

- Winning people over is not about manipulating people to like you, it's about giving people reasons to respect you.
- Leadership in the twenty-first century isn't about polish or precision or ego. It's about being authentic—the real you—and throwing your title out the door.
- You're going to need to show some heart. Care about how you lead, why you lead, and who you lead—and let that concern show.
- Get your hands dirty and show your team you're in this together. Stand up for your team, support them, and as often as possible, get in the trenches with them.

Walking the Plank

You can't ***win 'em over*** with every single decision you make. Why? Because the decisions that need to be made aren't always popular. Below, write the worst thing that could happen when you have to make an unpopular decision. Then, describe how you could minimize its impact.

Worst thing that could happen:

How you could minimize its impact:

Worst thing that could happen:

How you could minimize its impact:

Worst thing that could happen:

How you could minimize its impact:

Worst thing that could happen:

How you could minimize its impact:

Plan to Make Mistakes, but Not the Big Ones

WHAT ARE *THE* *big ones?* There's really only one—and that's tarnishing your reputation. Winning people over and convincing them that, no matter your age or background, you are a trustworthy leader, centers around just that—trust. As you read in the beginning of this section, although it can take a long time to build (or rebuild) your reputation, it doesn't take any time at all to destroy it.

So, think about the big picture. Make sure you are clear on your values, your intentions, and your word, and then keep all three safe. Still, no matter what happens, be ready to fix those errors you're inevitably going to make.

Damage Control

Imagine that something you've done (or are perceived to have done) or said (or someone thinks you said) has caused damage in each of these categories. Write how you could go about repairing and rebuilding each area in the eyes of your team, your supervisors, your colleagues, and even your own mind.

Trust

Confidence

Honesty

Dependability

Plan to Act

THE IDEA BEHIND this Leadership Planners series was never to solve your challenges. Rather, it was to help you sit down, lean back, look at them from new perspectives, and come up with a plan for improvement. This plan needs to be from you, for you, and by you so that it has a reasonable chance of fitting into your professional life and making a difference.

You've done a lot of work so far. You've considered victories, hurdles, risks, rewards, balance, support, communication, and promises. Before putting this book aside, you need to move your plan into action. Take a few moments now to review all of the work you've done so far and then come up with some real, concrete steps to take next.

Reading about a plan won't help. You need to plan to put it into action.

One Step at a Time

It's time to act. Be realistic but challenge yourself to take steps *now* to break down barriers to acceptance of your leadership. What will you do right away? What will you do very soon? And, finally, what will you do when the time is right?

3 When the Time Is Right	
2 Very Soon	
1 Right Away	

Sources

"4 Mistakes Not to Make When Managing Older Employees." *The Muse*. February 6, 2013. https://www.themuse.com/advice/4-mistakes-not-to-make-when-managing-older-employees.

Kratz, Harrison. "5 Tips for Establishing Yourself in The Office." *Work It Daily*. https://www.workitdaily.com/establishing-yourself-office-tips/.

Llopis, Glenn. "5 Ways Leaders Win People Over." *Forbes*. November 11, 2013. https://www.forbes.com/sites/glennllopis/2013/11/11/5-ways-leaders-win-people-over/#7d32cba43bd8.

"Managing Your Elders." EmploymentCrossing.com. May 14, 2012. https://www.employmentcrossing.com/article/231081/Managing-Your-Elders/.

Rosengren, Curt. "7 Ways to Make a Difference on the Job." *US News & World Report*. June 30, 2011. https://money.usnews.com/money/blogs/outside-voices-careers/2011/06/30/7-ways-to-make-a-difference-on-the-job.

Salemi, Vicki. "3 Things to Do ASAP When a Promotion Makes You the Boss of Your Friends." https://www.monster.com/career-advice/article/promotion-boss-of-friends/.

Wittenberg, Anka. "7 Ways to Help Boost Your Confidence at Work." *Entrepreneur*. August 11, 2015. https://www.entrepreneur.com/article/249428.

Notes